KATY PERRY

SINGING SENSATION

KATIE LAJINESS

Big Buddy Books
An Imprint of Abdo Publishing
abdopublishing.com

BIG
BUDDY POP BIOGRAPHIES

abdopublishing.com

Published by Abdo Publishing, a division of ABDO, PO Box 398166, Minneapolis, Minnesota 55439.
Copyright © 2016 by Abdo Consulting Group, Inc. International copyrights reserved in all countries.
No part of this book may be reproduced in any form without written permission from the publisher.
Big Buddy Books™ is a trademark and logo of Abdo Publishing.

Printed in the United States of America, North Mankato, Minnesota.
102015
012016

Cover Photo: Karwai Tang/Getty Images.
Interior Photos: Associated Press (pp. 9, 15, 17, 19, 23); CBS Photo Archive/Getty Images (p. 23);
    Lester Cohen/Getty Images (p. 11); Jeff Fusco/Getty Images (p. 13); Hulton Archive/Getty
    Images (p. 21); Jason LaVeris/Getty Images (p. 27); Kevin Mazur/Getty Images (pp. 25, 29);
    © Danny Moloshok/Reuters/Corbis (p. 5); Jordan Strauss/Invision/AP (p. 6); Toronto Star
    Archives/Getty Images (p. 21).

Coordinating Series Editor: Tamara L. Britton
Contributing Editor: Marcia Zappa
Graphic Design: Jenny Christensen

Library of Congress Cataloging-in-Publication Data

Lajiness, Katie, author.
  Katy Perry / Katie Lajiness.
     pages cm. -- (Big buddy pop biographies)
  Includes index.
  ISBN 978-1-68078-057-4
  1. Perry, Katy--Juvenile literature. 2. Singers--United States--Biography--Juvenile literature. I. Title.
  ML3930.P455L35 2016
  782.42164092--dc23
  [B]
                                    2015033031

CONTENTS

SINGING STAR

Katy Perry is a talented **pop** singer and songwriter. She has won **awards** for her hit albums and songs.

Katy has appeared on many magazine covers. And, she has been **interviewed** on popular television shows.

SNAPSHOT

NAME:
Katheryn Elizabeth
Hudson "Katy Perry"

BIRTHDAY:
October 25, 1984

BIRTHPLACE:
Santa Barbara, California

POPULAR ALBUMS:
One of the Boys,
Teenage Dream, Prism

FAMILY TIES

Katy Perry's real name is Katheryn Elizabeth Hudson. She was born in Santa Barbara, California, on October 25, 1984. Her parents are Keith and Mary Hudson. Katy's older sister is Angela. Her younger brother is David.

In 2014, Katy and her brother David Hudson attended the Grammy Awards.

WHERE IN THE WORLD?

Oregon
Idaho
Nevada
Utah
California
PACIFIC OCEAN
Santa Barbara
Arizona

GROWING UP

Growing up, Katy listened to **gospel** music. Katy's parents are **ministers**, and they **encouraged** her to sing in church.

Katy attended Dos Pueblos High School near Santa Barbara. She wanted to work in music. So, Katy left high school, and she earned a GED.

DID YOU KNOW

GED stands for General Educational Development. Students must take several tests to earn a GED. These tests measure the skills and knowledge comparable to a high school education.

Katy's parents, Keith Hudson *(left)* and Mary Hudson *(right)*, helped her get started as a singer.

STARTING OUT

Katy did not have an easy start in the music business. In 2001, she **released** a **Christian** album called *Katy Hudson*. It did not sell very well. But, Katy learned a lot about recording and the music business.

Katy worked hard to succeed in the music business. She learned by working with knowledgeable musicians, such as Glen Ballard.

BIG BREAK

Katy started to sing **pop** music. In 2008, she **released** her first pop album, *One of the Boys*. That same year, Katy was **nominated** for a **Grammy Award** for "I Kissed a Girl."

DID YOU KNOW
Katy wrote or helped write every song on *One of the Boys*.

Katy can play piano and guitar. In 2008, she played the guitar during her performance at the Jingle Ball in Camden, New Jersey.

TEENAGE DREAM

In May 2010, Katy **released** her second major album, *Teenage Dream*. "California Gurls," "E.T.," "Firework," "Last Friday Night (T.G.I.F.)," and "Teenage Dream" were popular songs from the album. They all went to number one on the charts! In 2010, she was **nominated** for four **Grammy Awards**.

DID YOU KNOW?
In 2011, Katy became the first woman to have five number-one songs from the same album!

Before long, Katy gained many fans! She often signed autographs for them.

As a **pop** star, Katy spends a lot of time on tour. She travels around the world to **perform** in front of her fans. From February 2011 to January 2012, Katy was on the California Dreams Tour. The tour was very successful!

During Katy's California Dreams Tour, she really charmed her fans. The show included rainbow stairs, giant candies, and a swing!

PRISM

In 2013, Katy **released** her third major album, *Prism*. Popular songs on the album included "Roar" and "Dark Horse." Both songs made it to the number-one spot on the charts!

In 2014, Katy sang her hit song "Roar" at the White House! She performed at an event hosted by President Barack Obama for the Special Olympics.

FASHION ICON

Katy is known for her fun fashion sense. She has an uncommon personal style. And, Katy often wears bright-colored wigs and unusual clothes.

Sometimes, people compare Katy's look to some beautiful 1930s and 1940s actresses. These women often appeared on posters called pinups.

Priscilla Lane *(left)* and Betty Grable *(below)* were famous pinup models. Katy's clothing and hair are often compared to their style.

A POP STAR'S LIFE

Katy is often on television shows. In 2010, she was a guest judge on *American Idol*.

Katy made a guest appearance on *How I Met Your Mother* in 2011. She won the 2012 People's Choice **Award** for Favorite TV Guest Star for her part!

In 2012, Katy **performed** on *American Idol* with **rapper** Kanye West. They sang a **remix** of "E.T."

Kanye West and Katy are both successful artists. In 2011, they won an MTV Video Award for "E.T."

Katy worked with actor Neil Patrick Harris on *How I Met Your Mother*. She played a character named Honey.

In addition to acting, Katy has also become a successful businesswoman. In 2010, Katy **released** a perfume called Purr. She put out many more perfumes with names such as Meowl, Oh So Sheer, and Mad Potion.

In June 2014, Katy started her own record label, **Metamorphosis** Music. She signed Ferras, a **pop**-rock singer.

Singer Ferras joined Katy on part of her Prismatic World Tour. They met in 2007 when they were both signed with Capitol Music Group.

AWARD WINNER

Katy is a powerful figure at **award** shows. People want to **interview** her on the red carpet.

Katy has had a winning career with many awards to her name. She has won five American Music Awards. And, Katy is a 14-time People's Choice Award winner!

In 2014, Katy won the MTV Video Music Award for Best Female Video. Her song "Dark Horse" featured rapper Juicy J.

BUZZ

DID YOU KNOW
Katy plans to release her fourth major album in 2016!

Katy was very busy in 2015! She traveled to many countries during her **Prismatic** World Tour. In February 2015, Katy sang at the Super Bowl. This is the National Football League's final game of the year. Millions of people watch every year.

Katy continues to be successful, and her **future** looks bright. Fans are excited to see what she does next!

More than 118 million people watched Katy sing during the Super Bowl halftime show. This was the most-watched halftime show ever!

GLOSSARY

award something that is given in recognition of good work or a good act.

Christian (KRIHS-chuhn) relating to Christianity, a religion that follows the teachings of Jesus Christ.

encourage to make more determined, hopeful, or confident.

future (FYOO-chuhr) a time that has not yet occurred.

gospel a type of Christian music.

Grammy Award any of the awards given each year by the National Academy of Recording Arts and Sciences. Grammy Awards honor the year's best accomplishments in music.

interview to ask someone a series of questions.

metamorphosis (meh-tuh-MAWR-fuh-suhs) changes that take place in some animals as they develop into adults.

minister a person who leads church worship.

nominate to name as a possible winner.

perform to do something in front of an audience.

pop relating to popular music.

prism (PRIH-zuhm) a block of glass cut in a special way that breaks light into a rainbow.

rapper someone who raps. To rap is to speak the words of a song to a beat.

release to make available to the public.

remix a new or different version of a recorded song that is made by changing or adding to the original recording of the song.

WEBSITES

To learn more about Pop Biographies, visit **booklinks.abdopublishing.com**. These links are routinely monitored and updated to provide the most current information available.

INDEX